What Is the

Written by Rozanne Lanczak Williams
Created by Sue Lewis
Illustrated by Patty Briles

Creative Teaching Press

What Is the Weather?
© 2002 Creative Teaching Press, Inc.
Written by Rozanne Lanczak Williams
Illustrated by Patty Briles
Project Manager: Sue Lewis
Project Director: Carolea Williams

Published in the United States of America by:
Creative Teaching Press, Inc.
P.O. Box 2723
Huntington Beach, CA 92647-0723

All rights reserved. No part of this book may be reproduced in any form without the written permission of Creative Teaching Press, Inc.

CTP 3232

What is the weather?

Too warm!

What is the weather?

Too windy!

What is the weather?

Too wet!

I wish the weather were...

wonderful!

Create your own book!

Cut a cloud-shaped cover and inside pages to make your own weather book. Use *w* words and other words you know to describe all types of weather. Illustrate the pages with cut paper collage pieces or watercolor paintings.

Words in *What Is the Weather?*

Initial Consonant: *w*
what
weather
warm
windy
wet
wish
were
wonderful

High-Frequency Words
is
the
too
I